Millionaire Mindset for Real Estate Success

Millionaire Mindset for Real Estate Success

Santosh Prasad Pal

First Printing, 2026

CONTENTS

This book is dedicated to my father Chandeshwar Prasad and mother Chayanmati Devi

1

Introduction

Build Millionaire Mindset before You Build Anything

Before you sell your first property. Before you build your first team. Before your bank account sees its first lakh—or its first crore. Before people recognize your name as a brand...There is something far more important you must build first. Your mindset.

Because real estate is not really a business of land, flats, or buildings. It is a business of belief, confidence, energy, persistence, and vision. Two agents may work in the same city. Same location. Same project. Same company. Yet one struggles month after month...While the other builds wealth, influence, and freedom. The difference is not luck. The difference is not talent. The difference is not timing. The difference is mindset.

This chapter will rewire the way you think—so you can rise as a top producer, a top earner, and eventually, a leader in real estate.

1. Winners Think Long-Term. Losers Think Only About Today.

Most people enter real estate with one expectation: "Fast money." When results don't come immediately...Motivation drops. Energy reduces. And slowly, they quit. But top-performing realtors play a very different game.

They focus on:

- Long-term relationships
- Long-term credibility
- Long-term brand building
- Long-term reputation

They understand one powerful truth:

Short-term thinking creates pressure whereas long-term thinking creates power.

If you want temporary income, think like a commission agent. If you want lasting success, think like a leader. Big success always belongs to those who are patient enough to build it.

2. Discipline Will Always Beat Talent

Real estate does not reward the smartest person in the room. It rewards the most consistent one. The most successful realtors follow boring but powerful daily habits:

- They wake up on time
- They plan their day with clarity
- They speak to 30–40 prospects every day
- They conduct site visits regularly
- They follow up relentlessly
- They keep learning
- They report their work honestly
- And they carry a zero-excuse mindset

People don't fail in real estate because they lack skill. They fail because they lack discipline. Talent may open the door. Discipline keeps it open forever.

3. Millionaire Realtors Think in Possibilities

Average realtors speak the language of excuses:
"Market slow hai."
"Client ka budget kam hai."
"Location bahut door hai."
"Log phone hi nahi uthate."
Millionaire realtors speak a different language:
"Slow market means less competition."
"If the dream is big, the budget can be planned."
"Every developing location carries future wealth."
"Every 'No' brings me closer to my 'Yes'."

The moment you stop complaining, and start reframing problems into opportunities—Your growth accelerates. Your reality always follows your thinking.

4. Growth Comes From Learning, Not Luck

Luck fades. Markets change. But learning compounds forever. The most successful real estate leaders are obsessive learners. They:

- Read books
- Attend training programs
- Study communication and psychology
- Master negotiation skills
- Know every project detail inside out
- Observe top performers closely

My own journey changed the day I decided to learn every single day—From mentors, from mistakes, from clients, and from the market itself. Learning places you miles ahead of 95% of the industry. In real estate, knowledge doesn't just create confidence—it creates conversion.

5. Rejection Is Not a Roadblock. It Is Training.

Every successful realtor has faced:

Rejected calls

Cancelled meetings

No-show site visits

“Budget nahi hai” buyers

“Kal call kariyega” excuses

Rejection is not here to break you. Rejection is here to build you. Each rejection teaches:

- How to qualify better
- How to communicate smarter
- How to follow up effectively
- How to stay emotionally strong
- How to sell with confidence, not desperation

You never fail when a customer says no. You fail only when you stop believing in yourself.

6. High Energy Creates High Sales

Real estate is not a logic business alone. It is an energy business. People don't just buy property. They buy confidence. They buy from agents who carry:

- High energy
- Positive thinking
- Clear communication
- Strong belief

A low-energy agent cannot sell even the best project. A high-energy agent can sell average property with conviction. Your energy enters the room before your words do. Before you sell a property—Sell your confidence.

7. The Habit of Massive Action

Most people analyze. Some people plan. Very few people act. Action creates income. Millionaire realtors live by one rule: Act fast.

They improve on the way. They make the call, visit the site, meet the client, send the message, attend the event, post on social media, follow up again and again.

These action kills fear. It creates momentum and momentum creates money. Massive action always leads to massive income.

8. Serve Big, and Money Will Follow

One of the biggest traps in real estate: Chasing commission.

Top performers focus on something else:

- Customer trust
- Customer clarity
- Customer dreams
- Customer experience

When you genuinely serve— When you guide honestly— When you advise professionally—Money automatically follows you. Clients may forget the flat number...But they never forget how you made them feel. Service builds income. Trust builds legacy.

9. Your Environment Will Decide Your Income

Success is contagious—and so is failure. If you sit with negative people your confidence drops and same is true for average people your thinking stays average.

High achievers your standards rise. Choose your environment wisely. Work under strong leaders. Spend time with top performers. Network with successful developers. Join growth-driven communities like BNI and build relationships with ambitious minds. In real estate, your network often decides your net worth.

10. Believe That You Deserve Success

The deepest secret of the millionaire mindset is simple:

- They believe they deserve success.
- They expect respect.
- They expect abundance.
- They expect growth.

When your belief rises, your actions rise. When your actions rise, your results rise. Never shrink your dreams to match your reality. Expand your reality to match your dreams. Believe you can. Believe you deserve. Believe you will.

Reflection:

Every breakthrough in real estate begins in the mind. Mindset creates discipline. Discipline creates action. Action creates results. Results build confidence. Confidence creates massive success

Projects will come and go. Markets will rise and fall. But a millionaire mindset will win in any condition. Your real estate journey does not start outside. It begins inside your mind.

2

The Genesis of a Real Estate Champion

"You have to dream before your dreams can come true."
- Dr. A.P.J. Abdul Kalam

Every success story has a beginning. Some beginnings are loud, some are dramatic, and some are silent. My journey began silently—with dreams bigger than my circumstances, with responsibilities heavier than my shoulders, and with a determination stronger than my challenges. I did not choose real estate. Real estate chose me.

Roots That Built the Foundation

I was born in Bihar—where values are strong, families are close, and dreams are often bigger than the opportunities available. Growing up, I understood early what struggle looks like, what responsibility feels like, and what ambition demands.

My childhood was simple but filled with curiosity. Even as a young boy, I loved observing people—how they spoke, how they made decisions, how they negotiated. At that time, I didn't know these qualities would one day become my biggest strengths in real estate.

After completing my schooling in Bihar, I moved to Delhi-NCR for further studies. This move opened my mind. New faces, new culture, new competition—it shaped my attitude towards growth. Later, I went to Odisha for my master's degree. Education became my stepping stone, but destiny had a different plan for me.

The Corporate Journey: Chandigarh → Nashik → Indore → Dewas

Before stepping into real estate, I built my life in the pharmaceutical industry.

My first step was Chandigarh

A new city, a new job, a new struggle. I worked hard, learned corporate communication, discipline, process management, and how to approach people with confidence. Then came Nashik, where I began understanding markets more deeply — demand, supply, customer psychology.

Later, I moved to Indore, working with Cipla Limited. This city gave me stability, but it also reminded me of my dreams.

Finally, I joined my dream company — Ranbaxy in Dewas. Most people would have settled there. But my heart wanted something more meaningful, more impactful, more challenging. I wanted to build something of my own. Something that created jobs. Something that improved people's lives. Something that fulfilled dreams.

The Turning Point: Entering Real Estate

Around 2018, I noticed something powerful:

People were buying land not just for living...But for security, growth, respect, and future planning.

I met families who were searching for honest guidance. I met youngsters who wanted opportunities but lacked direction. I met investors who were ready to grow but needed trustworthy advisors. This was the moment. This was the calling.

With zero background, zero team, and zero project of my own —I entered the world of real estate. Many people laughed. Some doubted. Some discouraged. But I had three unshakable things:

1. Belief in myself
2. Hard work without excuses
3. Commitment to serve honestly

And these three things are enough to rewrite a person's destiny.

The Struggle Phase: The Real Test

The early days were the toughest. No leads. No closing. No team. No investors.

No overnight success. Every morning started with hope. Every night ended with tired feet—but a strong heart. Some days, people didn't pick calls. Some days, customers said "I will think." Some days, I returned home without any result. But every day taught me something. I learned:

- How to talk with confidence
- How to build trust
- How to show plots effectively
- How to handle rejections
- How to understand what a customer really wants
- How to stay motivated when everything is going wrong

Slowly, very slowly... I started growing. One booking... then another... then a few more. The seed had finally started growing into a plant.

The Rise of a Vision: From Agent to Entrepreneur

As results increased, so did responsibilities. I started training people. I started building a small team. I started improving systems. After a few years, I partnered in multiple successful offices. More families trusted me. More customers recommended me. And then came the biggest step of my life...

Birth of Indore Property Management Pvt. Ltd. (IPM)

I decided to create a company that represented:

- Transparency
- Trust
- Professionalism
- Systematic Growth
- Customer-first service

This is how Indore Property Management Pvt. Ltd. (IPM) was born. From one person to a team of 60+ strong professionals, from zero to 16+ active projects, from a few customers to 2,500+ happy families, from renting a table to launching multiple branch offices...IPM became a symbol of hard work, honesty, and unstoppable growth.

The Secret Behind the Success

People often ask: "What is the real secret behind your success?"
And I always say:

- Success is not built in a day. It is built every day.
- When you refuse to quit, success has no option but to come to you.

- Real estate rewards those who stay consistent.

My success is not magic. It is the result of:

- continuous learning
- discipline
- patience
- passion
- helping others grow

Real estate changed my life. And now, through this book, it will change yours too. Because this chapter of my life reveals:

- Every champion has a beginning.
- Your beginning may look small today...
- But your future can be unlimited.

If I can do it with no background, no money, no godfather — then you can do it too.

Reflection:

This chapter is not just my story. It is proof that...Real estate is the most powerful opportunity in India. And you are one decision away from changing your life.

Action Points:

1. Start from where you are—no excuses.
2. Build belief before expecting results.
3. Learn by observing people and situations.
4. Treat struggle as training, not failure.

5. Improve communication and confidence daily.
6. Be honest and customer-focused.
7. Stay patient and consistent.
8. Think long-term, not just quick deals.
9. Never quit, even when progress is slow.

3

The Millionaire Mindset for Real Estate

*"Selling is not about convincing people. It is about understanding people." - **Philip Kotler***

Real estate is not a business of land and buildings. It is a business of confidence, belief, energy, persistence, and vision. The difference between a struggling realtor and a successful realtor is not location, project, company or luck. The difference is mindset. This chapter will teach you the mindset that creates top producers, top earners, and top leaders.

1. Winners Think Long-Term. Losers Think Today Only

Most people enter real estate expecting quick money.
And when results take time, they quit.
But top real estate performers focus on:

- Long-term relationships
- Long-term growth
- Long-term brand building
- Long-term reputation

They understand:

- Short-term thinking gives stress.
- Long-term thinking gives success.

If you want to grow big, start thinking like a leader—not like a commission agent.

2. Discipline Beats Talent

Real estate doesn't reward the smartest person. It rewards the most consistent person. Successful realtors follow daily discipline:

- Wake up early
- Plan the day
- Talk to minimum 30–40 prospects
- Site visits
- Follow-ups
- Learning
- Daily reporting
- Zero excuse attitude

Realtors don't fail because of lack of skill. They fail because of lack of discipline. Remember, talent can start your journey but discipline will finish it.

3. A Millionaire Realtor Has a Possibility Mindset

Average realtors think:

1. "Market slow hai."
2. "Customer budget se bahar hai."
3. "Location door hai."

4. "Log call nahi uthate."

Millionaire realtors think:

1. "Slow market = less competition = more opportunity."
2. "If customer has a dream, budget will adjust."
3. "Location is an opportunity to explain future growth."
4. "Every NO is a step to my YES."

Your success starts when you stop complaining and start converting every problem into an opportunity.

4. Growth Comes from Learning, Not Luck

The most successful real estate leaders in the world are obsessive learners.

- They read books.
- They attend training.
- They improve communication.
- They learn project details deeply.
- They learn negotiation and psychology.
- They observe top performers.

My own growth happened because I learned every day—through experience, training, mistakes, and real market situations. Learning keeps you ahead of 95% of the industry.

5. Rejections Are Not Roadblocks—They Are Milestones

Every great realtor you know has faced:

1. Rejected calls

2. Cancelled meetings
3. No-shows on site visits
4. "Budget nahi hai" customers
5. "Aap kal call kariyega" customers

Rejection is not your enemy. Rejection is your training partner. Each rejection teaches you:

1. How to talk better
2. How to identify real buyers
3. How to follow up smarter
4. How to present with confidence
5. How to stay emotionally strong

You don't fail in real estate when customers reject you.
You fail only when you reject yourself.

6. High Energy = High Sales
Real estate is an energy business. People buy from people with:

1. High confidence
2. High positivity
3. High enthusiasm
4. High clarity

A low-energy agent cannot sell even the best property. But a high-energy agent can sell even average property.

Your energy is your currency. Your energy decides your income. Before selling a plot, sell your confidence.

7. The Habit of Taking Massive Action

Most people think. Only a few take action. And only action creates income. Millionaire realtors have these rules:

- They don't wait.
- Don't think too much.
- Take action immediately.
- Make calls.
- Visit sites.
- Meet people.
- Send messages.
- Attend events.
- Promote on social media.
- Show property.
- Follow up again and again.

Massive action = Massive income.

8. Focus on Service, Money Will Follow

The biggest mistake new realtors make: Focusing only on commission.

Top realtors focus on:

- Customer trust
- Customer experience
- Customer needs
- Customer dreams

When you serve honestly, passionately and professionally...Money will automatically chase you. People don't remember the plot you showed. They remember how you made them feel. Serve big, earn big.

9. Your Environment Shapes Your Success

Your success depends on who you spend time with:

1. If you sit with negative people → you will lose confidence.
2. If you sit with average people → you will stay average.
3. If you sit with winners → you will become unstoppable.

Work under good leaders. Stay around high performers. Learn from successful developers. Join growth-oriented networks (like BNI). Build relationships with ambitious people. Real estate is a relationship-driven industry. Choose your environment carefully.

10. Believe You Deserve Success

The biggest secret of millionaire mindset:

- They believe they deserve success.
- They believe they deserve respect.
- They believe they deserve abundance.

When you expect greatness, your actions become great. When your actions become great, your results become great. Believe you can. Believe you deserve. Believe you will.

Reflection:

Success in real estate starts with success in your mind. If your mindset is strong, your skills automatically grow. If your mindset is weak, even the best project cannot help you.

Remember:

1. Mindset creates discipline
2. Discipline creates action
3. Action creates results
4. Results create confidence
5. Confidence creates massive success

Your millionaire journey starts inside your mind.

Action Points:

1. **Think Long-Term**
   Focus on relationships, reputation, and brand—not quick commissions.
2. **Follow Daily Discipline**
   Fixed routine, daily calls, follow-ups, learning, and zero excuses.
3. **Convert Problems into Opportunities**
   Stop complaining about market, budget, or location—start reframing them.
4. **Learn Every Day**
   Invest time in books, training, communication, and market knowledge.
5. **Treat Rejection as Feedback**
   Every "no" improves your confidence, clarity, and conversion skills.
6. **Maintain High Energy**
   Your confidence and enthusiasm directly impact your sales results.

7. **Serve First, Earn Later**
   When you focus on customer trust and experience, money follows automatically.

4

Understanding Market Cycles

"The key to making money in real estate is not timing the market perfectly, but understanding where the market is headed."- ***Sam Zell (Legendary Real Estate Investor)***

Real estate is like nature—It has seasons, patterns, rhythms and cycles. A successful realtor does not depend on luck. A successful realtor understands when to buy, when to sell, where to invest, and how to predict future growth.

If you understand market cycles... You will never fear slowdowns. You will never miss opportunities. You will always stay ahead of 95% of realtors. This chapter reveals the complete science of real estate cycles—explained simply, practically, and with real examples.

The 4 Major Real Estate Cycles

Every city—Indore, Dewas, Pune, Bangalore, Delhi—goes through the same 4 cycles:

1. Expansion Phase
2. Boom Phase
3. Stabilization Phase
4. Correction Phase

Master these cycles and you will master real estate forever.

1. Expansion Phase (Best Time for Buyers, Investors & New Realtors)

This is the phase when a location starts growing. Infrastructure is being planned or silently developing:

1. New roads announced
2. Ring road proposals
3. Airport expansion
4. Metro or BRTS planning
5. Big education institutions
6. IT parks being planned
7. Major builders buying land
8. Industries coming nearby

Prices are affordable. But future potential is massive.

Signs of Expansion Phase:

- Plots available at low to medium prices
- Early investors and visionaries entering
- Government announcements but not completed yet
- Builders silently acquiring land
- Development work starting slowly

Why This Phase Is a Goldmine? Because smart people enter early. Example: Ujjain Road, Super Corridor, MR-10, TCS area — years ago these places were empty...Today they are booming.

This is the phase where people become:

- Future millionaires

- Long-term investors
- Early project leaders

2. Boom Phase (Fastest Profit Phase)

In this phase, the location becomes HOT. Everyone starts talking about it.

1. Roads are completed
2. Big brands enter
3. New townships start
4. Population increases
5. Rental demand rises
6. Land value jumps rapidly
7. Builders launch premium projects

Signs of Boom Phase

- Prices rise every 3–6 months
- High demand, low supply
- Investors selling at 40%–200% profit
- Many realtors enter suddenly
- Customers fear missing out

This Phase Creates Maximum Millionaires. If you have inventory in boom phase, then you will earn the highest commissions. If you own land, you will see magic-level appreciation. But you must also prepare for the next phase.

3. Stabilization Phase (Balanced Market Phase)

This is the phase when the prices stop rising sharply. The market becomes stable.

- Demand is steady
- Supply becomes balanced
- Prices rise slowly
- Investors become selective
- End-users dominate the market

Signs of Stabilization

- Prices stay same for months
- Sales continue but at normal speed
- Heavy competition among realtors
- Quality of projects improves
- Builders add amenities to attract end-users

This Phase Is Best For:

1. End users
2. Long-term investors
3. Developers launching mid-budget homes

Stabilization is healthy.
It creates trust and attracts genuine buyers.

4. Correction Phase (Not a Crash. A Natural Pause.)

Correction is misunderstood. People think correction = danger. But actually, correction is like:

- Rain after summer
- Rest after hard work
- A pause before next growth cycle

Signs of Correction
- Buyers become cautious
- Investors slow down
- Some projects delay
- Prices stop increasing
- Market waits for next trigger

Why Correction Is Normal?

Every industry has corrections: gold, stock market, IT, agriculture, everything. Real estate corrections create:

- New opportunities
- Affordable entry points
- Cleaner, more transparent markets

Smart Realtors Use This Phase To:
- Train more
- Acquire more knowledge
- Build relationships
- Prepare for expansion phase
- Buy and hold inventory

This phase separates weak realtors who quit with the strong ones who grows.

How to Predict the Next Big Location

These are the 6 signals I personally use at IPM:

1. Government Projects like roads, bridges, ring road, BRTS, airports, metro lines where the government invests and growth follows.

2. Corporate & Industrial Entry. If IT companies, MNCs, logistics parks, industries plan land, then prices jump in 1–2 years.

3. Education & Healthcare Expansion. Universities, medical colleges, big schools raise land value within 5 km.

4. Builder Movement. When big developers silently buy land. They already know the future.

5. Big Township Announcements. Townships attract money, population, infrastructure, and appreciation.

6. Connectivity Boost. A location with great connectivity grows unstoppable:

- Ring road
- National highway
- Airport road
- Metro stations
- Major commercial hubs

Wherever connectivity improves, rates jump there.

The 5-year Pattern You Must Understand

Most locations follow this pattern:

- Years 1–2: Expansion (Early Investors enter)
- Year 3: Boom (Prices rise fast)
- Year 4: Stabilization (Market matures)
- Year 5: Correction (Short pause → again Expansion starts)

This cycle keeps repeating. If you understand this—you will always sell smartly.

What Smart Realtors do in Each Phase

Expansion Phase:

- Buy land

- Promote vision
- Build network
- Sell future potential

Boom Phase:

- Sell fast
- Build brand
- Acquire more projects
- Maximize income

Stabilization Phase:

- Focus on service
- Target end-users
- Launch mid-budget projects
- Improve customer relationships

Correction Phase

- Prepare for next cycle
- Invest personally
- Train team
- Strengthen systems
- Study market deeply

This is how experts stay ahead. This is how IPM grew even during slowdowns.

Reflection:

Market cycles are not problems. They are patterns that help you make smart decisions. If you understand cycles:

- You will invest wisely
- You will sell powerfully
- You will handle slowdowns confidently
- You will identify the next big location
- You will become a leader, not just an agent

Real estate rewards people who understand timing. This chapter gives you the timing blueprint.

Action Points:

1. **Identify the Current Market Phase**
   Always analyze whether the location is in expansion, boom, stabilization, or correction.
2. **Enter Early, Exit Smart**
   Buy or promote aggressively in expansion and boom; plan exits before saturation.
3. **Track Government & Infrastructure Signals**
   Follow road, metro, airport, and township announcements to predict growth.
4. **Observe Builder & Corporate Movement**
   Where big developers and companies move, future appreciation follows.
5. **Adjust Strategy in Every Cycle**
   Change your selling, investing, and marketing approach according to the phase.

6. **Use Slow Markets to Prepare**
   During correction, focus on learning, relationship building, and system strengthening.
7. **Think in 5-Year Vision, Not Monthly Sales**
   Real wealth in real estate is created by understanding long-term cycle

5

Become the Most Trusted Brand in Real Estate

"People do not buy goods and services. They buy trust, confidence, and relationships."- ***Seth Godin From Unknown to Unstoppable***

Brand is not your logo. Brand is not your company. Brand is what people say about you when you are not in the room. In the real estate industry, your brand is your currency.

Trust = Deals.

Credibility = Conversions.

Reputation = Long-term Success.

In this chapter, we will uncover the complete science of brand building — the exact process top realtors, developers, and property consultants use to become the first choice in their market.

4.1 Why Brand Matters More Than Experience

In real estate, customers don't select the most experienced person...They select the most trusted person. A strong brand helps you:

- Attract more clients
- Close deals faster

- Charge better commissions
- Build long-term reputation
- Become the first call for referrals
- Stand out even in a crowded marketplace

When customers feel safe with you, they don't negotiate much. They follow your guidance. They bring their friends and family. A powerful brand turns you from an agent into an authority.

4.2 The 7 Pillars of Personal Branding in Real Estate

To build a brand that lasts, you must master these seven pillars:

1. Identity

Who are you and why should people trust you?

Examples:

• "Plot & Villa Expert – Ujjain Road & Super Corridor Specialists"

• "Affordable Housing Consultant – Indore"

• "Luxury Property Advisor – Central India"

Specialization increases authority.

2. Appearance & Presence

How you present yourself shapes perceptions:

• Dress well, in clean professional outfits

• Maintain proper grooming

• Carry a confident but humble posture

In real estate, appearance is an asset — it communicates success and reliability.

3. Online Visibility

People MUST find you easily on:

• Facebook

• Instagram

• YouTube

• Google
• WhatsApp Business
• LinkedIn

If you are not online, you don't exist in today's real estate market.

4. Content Strategy

Your content should include:

- Market updates
- Property demos
- Customer testimonials
- Construction status videos
- Educational posts
- Real estate tips
- Lifestyle and motivation content

Content = Authority.

Authority = Trust.

Trust = Sales.

5. Consistency

The biggest branding mistake? Posting today, disappearing tomorrow.

Your brand grows when you:

• Post daily
• Meet new people every week
• Share achievements regularly
• Update your projects consistently

Consistency builds memory.

6. Social Proof

People don't trust what you say...they trust what others say about you.

Collect and showcase:

- Video testimonials
- Written reviews
- Photo proof
- Project handovers
- Client selfies
- Group photos

Social proof = Instant trust.

7. Storytelling

Your journey is the heart of your brand.

Example: "How I started with zero experience and today manage 21+ projects and a 90+ member team..."

People connect with stories, not sales pitches.

4.3 Digital Branding Tools You Must Use

WhatsApp Business Mastery

Create a premium profile with:

- Display picture
- Catalog of projects
- Welcome message
- Quick replies
- Status updates
- Auto-responses

Your WhatsApp is your digital office.

Instagram Growth System

Your Instagram reflects your lifestyle & success.

Post categories:

- Reels (property tours, motivation, success stories)
- Carousels (project features, tips)
- Stories (daily updates, meetings, site visits)
- Highlights (testimonials, tours, projects)

Your Instagram must show:

- Success
- Activity
- Knowledge
- Professionalism

YouTube Authority Building

Why YouTube? Because it creates long-term trust.

Video ideas:

- Project walkthroughs
- Buying guides
- Plot investment strategies
- Customer success stories
- Live Q&A
- Drone view of projects

YouTube = Education + Trust.

4.4 Offline Branding: Be Unforgettable

Strong offline branding helps you convert walk-ins into bookings.

Essential Branding Assets:

- Visiting Card
- Property Brochures
- Standee
- Glow Sign Boards
- Polo T-Shirts
- Caps
- Office Branding
- Car Branding
- ID Cards
- Team Uniform

- Banner Boards at sites

When people see your brand everywhere, they remember you.

4.5 The Psychology of Brand Trust

Trust is built through:

1. Transparency

Clear communication about prices, documents, timelines.

2. Honesty

If a project is not right for a customer, say it.

3. Knowledge

People trust experts, not sellers.

4. Confidence

Speak with clarity, calmness, and conviction.

5. Professionalism

- Arrive on time.
- Dress well.
- Communicate clearly.
- Follow commitments.

Professional behavior is branding in action.

4.6 Brand Positioning Formula (IPM Style)

To position yourself uniquely:

Step 1: Choose your niche

(IPM Example: Ujjain Road + Super Corridor Specialist)

Step 2: Create a tagline

"Helping families find peace, progress, and property."

Step 3: Build your signature style

• Language

- Behavior
- Approach

Step 4: Show results

Your achievements define your authority.

4.7 Mistakes That Destroy Branding

- Focusing only on selling
- Using low-quality photos/videos
- Negative talk about competitors
- No consistency
- Fake promises
- Overposting personal drama
- Cheap marketing
- Lack of communication
- No follow-up
- Not investing in self-growth

Brand is fragile — protect it at all costs.

4.8 Case Study: How I Built the IPM Brand

Your own real-life journey becomes a powerful lesson:

- Starting alone to leading a team of 90+
- Managing 21+ residential projects
- Helping 7500+ families
- Organizing mega events, blood donation drives, and social services
- Launching multiple projects in different locations simultaneously
- Building IPM Seva Foundation
- Becoming trusted for "Monopoly Projects" in Indore & Dewas

Your commitment, consistency, and community service built your brand — not just your sales.

4.9 Your Branding Action Plan (30 Days)

Week 1: Foundation

- Create your niche
- Make your digital cards
- Update your Instagram bio
- Set up WhatsApp Business

Week 2: Visibility

- Post 10 reels
- Share 10 stories
- Meet 10 new customers

Week 3: Authority

- Record 3 testimonials
- Publish 3 property tours
- Write 5 tips on real estate

Week 4: Growth

- Organize a mini-event
- Do live Q&A
- Collaborate with other influencers

Do this for 30 days — your brand will explode.

4.10 Conclusion: Brand is Your Legacy

Properties will change. Projects will come and go. Markets will rise and fall. But your brand stays forever. Your brand is your signature. Your identity. Your power.

Your future. Build it like a temple. Protect it like a treasure. Grow it like a mission. Because in real estate, people don't invest in property first...Thcy invest in YOU.

Action Points:

1. **Choose a Clear Niche**
   Decide what you want to be known for—location, segment, or specialization.
2. **Be Visible Everywhere**
   Stay active online and offline so people recognize and remember you easily.
3. **Create Value-Driven Content**
   Educate, guide, and inform instead of only selling properties.
4. **Stay Consistent Daily**
   Regular posting, follow-ups, and communication build strong brand recall.
5. **Show Social Proof Boldly**
   Display testimonials, client success stories, and real results to build instant trust.
6. **Act Professionally at All Times**
   Your behavior, communication, and honesty define your brand more than marketing.
7. **Think Long-Term, Not Transactional**
   Focus on relationships and reputation—money will follow naturally .

6

Generate Unlimited Leads & Maximum Visibility

"Marketing creates visibility. Visibility creates trust.Trust creates sales." - ***Santosh Prasad Pal***

Marketing is the heart of real estate.

Sales happen only when your marketing creates trust, demand, and desire. Most agents try to "sell" properties, while successful realtors market themselves so powerfully that customers come searching for them.

In this chapter, we will unlock the complete Marketing Mastery System — a step-by-step playbook used by top-performing property consultants, brokers, and developers.

5.1 Why Marketing is the King in Real Estate

Real estate is a competition-heavy market. Thousands of agents, hundreds of builders, dozens of projects.

If your marketing is strong, you stand out. If your marketing is weak, you disappear. Marketing helps you:

- Generate unlimited leads
- Create massive visibility

- Build trust before selling
- Educate customers
- Position yourself as an expert
- Increase your closing ratio
- Grow your income exponentially

Marketing is not an expense. It is an investment that multiplies your business.

5.2 The 3 Golden Principles of Real Estate Marketing

1. Visibility → Credibility → Profitability

If people don't see you, they won't trust you. If they don't trust you, they won't call you. If they don't call you, they won't buy from you.

2. Consistency Beats Talent

Posting once and waiting won't work. Marketing is a daily task — just like eating, sleeping, and breathing.

3. Emotions Sell, Not Features

People buy homes based on:

- Family needs
- Dreams
- Security
- Lifestyle

Marketing must touch emotions, not just show buildings.

5.3 The 10-Pillar Marketing System (IPM Formula)

Here are the pillars to dominate real estate marketing:

Pillar 1: Social Media Dominance

Your goal is simple:

Be seen everywhere.

Focus platforms:

- Instagram
- Facebook
- YouTube
- WhatsApp
- LinkedIn
- Google Business Profile

Your content must show:

- Property education
- Market updates
- Success stories
- Site visit videos
- Drone shots
- Testimonials
- Project highlights
- Motivational thoughts

Social media = modern real estate office.

Pillar 2: Reels & Short Videos

Reels are the king of reach. People love short, fast, informative videos.

Content Ideas:

- 30-second property tour
- Before/after development
- 3 reasons to buy this location
- Plot investment tip
- Myth vs Reality
- Client handover clip

Reels increase your identity faster than anything.

Pillar 3: WhatsApp Business Marketing

WhatsApp = Direct Connection.

Use it to:

- Broadcast offers
- Share status updates
- Send catalogs
- Follow up leads
- Build relationship

Your WhatsApp DP, bio, stories, greeting message — everything matters.

Pillar 4: Google Business Profile (Most Underrated!)

Google helps customers nearby find you easily. Update:

- Location
- Working hours
- Photos
- Reviews
- Project details

People trust Google reviews more than verbal promises.

Pillar 5: Offline Branding Power

Use:

- Flex banners
- Road signs near project
- Auto rickshaw ads
- Bus stop boards
- Flyers
- Hoardings

Offline + Online = Maximum impact.

Pillar 6: Event-Based Marketing

Events create urgency & excitement. Example events:

- Project Launch
- Site Visit Evening
- Customer Appreciation Day
- Brokers Meet
- Blood Donation Drive (Brand + Humanity)
- Free Investment Seminar

These events-brand you as a leader, not just a seller.

Pillar 7: Locality Targeting Strategy

Instead of targeting the whole city, target specific areas. Target by:

- Income group
- Family size
- Job location
- Lifestyle
- Budget

Targeted marketing = higher conversions.

Pillar 8: Relationship-Based Marketing

Real estate grows fastest through relationships. Build networks with:

- BNI
- Builders
- Brokers
- Lawyers
- Bankers
- CA
- NRI Investors

Your network = your net worth.

Pillar 9: Education-Based Marketing

People trust those who teach them. Create:

- Free seminars
- Online webinars
- Buyer's guide PDF
- Investment calculator
- Legal checklist

When you educate, customers automatically follow you.

Pillar 10: Follow-Up Marketing System

Rich agents follow up. Poor agents give up. Use:

- Automated messages
- Follow-up scripts
- WhatsApp reminders
- Personal calls
- Festival greetings

Follow-up = Money.

5.4 The Real Estate Marketing Funnel (Step-by-Step)

Step 1 – Awareness

Reels, flyers, YouTube, Google, reels.

Step 2 – Interest

Property videos, offers, highlights.

Step 3 – Engagement

WhatsApp chats, consultation calls, brochures.

Step 4 – Site Visit

Personalized experience.

Step 5 – Conversion

Booking + paperwork.

Marketing brings them into the funnel whereas sales converts them.

5.5 Emotional Triggers That Make Clients Act

Human decisions are emotional. Use these triggers:

- "Limited plots available"
- "Last chance to get pre-launch price"
- "Best location for your children's future"
- "Safe investment for long-term growth"
- "Only few corner plots left"

Emotions move customers faster than logic.

5.6 Mistakes That Kill Marketing

- Posting without consistency
- Focusing only on selling
- Copying others instead of building your style
- Ignoring Google reviews
- Low-quality videos
- Not creating urgency
- Zero follow-up
- Not investing in paid ads
- No clear target audience

Marketing must be strategic — not random.

5.7 30-Day Real Estate Marketing Action Plan

Week 1

- Set up all social media profiles
- Create brand templates
- Shoot 10 reels
- Collect 5 testimonials

Week 2

- Run Google ads (₹300–₹500/day)
- Publish 4 detailed videos
- Daily WhatsApp status updates

Week 3

- Weekly event at the project
- Add 50 new contacts
- 10 collaborations with local businesses

Week 4

- Launch your personal newsletter
- Publish a "Market Report"
- Run a referral campaign

Do this for 30 days → your leads will explode.

5.8 Conclusion: Marketing Creates Wealth

In real estate, sales give you income, and marketing builds your business. A great product fails without marketing, but even an average product sells with powerful marketing. If you apply this chapter, your brand, reach, and income will multiply.

Marketing is not magic. It is a system — a system that works for those who work it.

Action Points

1. **Focus on Marketing Before Selling**
   Build visibility and trust first—sales will follow naturally.
2. **Be Visible Every Single Day**
   Show up consistently on social media, WhatsApp, Google, and on-ground.
3. **Use Emotion-Based Marketing**
   Sell dreams, security, and lifestyle—not just property features.

4. **Master Short-Form Video Content**
   Reels and short videos are the fastest way to gain reach and authority.
5. **Create a Strong Follow-Up System**
   Consistent follow-ups convert interest into bookings.
6. **Combine Online and Offline Marketing**
   Digital visibility plus local presence creates maximum impact.
7. **Treat Marketing as a Daily Habit**
   Marketing is not a campaign—it is a system you must run every day.

7

Sales and Closing Mastery

"The aim of marketing is to know and understand the customer so well that the product or service fits him and sells itself."- ***Peter Drucker***

Turn Every Lead Into a Loyal Buyer. Sales is not about forcing customers to buy. Sales is about guiding customers to make the right decision. The top real estate closers are not the best talkers...They are the best listeners, problem-solvers, and trust builders. This chapter is your complete blueprint to becoming a master closer.

6.1 The Mindset of a Sales Champion

Before closing deals, you must build the right mindset.
A sales master believes:

- "I am a problem-solver, not a seller."
- "Every customer wants the right property. I help them find it."
- "Follow-up is respect, not pressure."
- "People buy confidence—so I must become confident."

Sales = Mindset + Skill + System.

6.2 The 3-Stage Real Estate Sales System (IPM Formula)

There are only 3 stages:

Stage 1 – Connection

Build rapport and trust within the first 2 minutes.

Ask questions like:

- "Aap kitne time se property explore kar rahe hain?"
- "Aapka main purpose kya hai—investment ya ghar banana?"

Connection → Comfort → Conversion.

Stage 2 – Qualification

Your goal is to understand their exact needs.

Ask:

- Location preference
- Budget
- Family size
- Purpose (investment, rental, residence)
- Future plan
- Time to buy

Qualification saves time, builds trust, and helps you pitch the right property.

Stage 3 – Presentation & Closing

Show the property that matches their dream. Explain benefits, not features.

And then guide them confidently to the booking.

Presentation → Persuasion → Payment.

6.3 The Psychology Behind Why People Buy Property

Customers buy property for following emotional reasons:

- Safety of family
- Stability

- Growth of investment
- Better lifestyle
- Peace of mind
- Security of future
- Children's future

If you connect to their emotions, they buy faster.

6.4 The Ultimate IPM Closing Script (Works 95% of Time)

Use this step-by-step closing script:

- "Aapko location kaisi lag rahi hai?"
- "Budget aapke range me comfortably aa raha hai?"
- "Aapko 2 options dikha raha hoon—corner ya east-facing."
- "Aapki family ko kaunsa pasand aayega?"
- "Aap booking today karna chahte hain ya tomorrow morning? Dono okay."

This script gives choice, not pressure. Customers love it.

6.5 Techniques of Master Closers

Technique 1: Silent Close

After showing the best plot... stay silent. Silence creates pressure → customer speaks → decision emerges.

Technique 2: Comparison Close

"Sir, 3 mahine pehle yahi plot 500 rs kam tha... abhi 30 customers pooch chuke hain."

People hate missing out.

Technique 3: Emotional Close

"This plot aapke bachchon ke future ke liye perfect hai."

Technique 4: Urgency Close

"Only 2 units left in this lane—after this price will jump."

Technique 5: Trust Close

"Sir, main aapko wahi suggest kar raha hoon jo main apne bhai ko suggest karta."

Trust closes deals.

6.6 The Perfect Site Visit Strategy

Your site visit must be an experience, not a tour.

Before Visit:

- Google location pin
- Project details
- Payment plan
- FAQs

During Visit:

- Greet warmly
- Show the best route
- Start with the best plots
- Speak confident & slow
- Talk less, listen more

After Visit:

- Send thank you message
- Share availability
- Create urgency
- Follow-up next morning

Site Visit → Emotion → Booking.

6.7 Follow-Up: The Real Money Maker

80% sales happen after the 5th follow-up.
Follow-up examples:

- "Sir, a quick update—3 plots booked today."
- "Aapke favorite plot ka price increase notice aaya hai."
- "Aaj site visit free hai. Aap aa sakte ho kya?"

Never follow up to "force". Follow up to inform and guide.

6.8 The 5 Reasons Clients Don't Buy — And How to Fix Them

- Confusion → Give clarity
- Overthinking → Create urgency
- Budget mismatch → Show range options
- Family pressure → Offer family visit
- Trust issue → Show testimonials + documents

Every objection has a solution.

6.9 Conclusion: Closing is a Daily Habit

A master closer:

- Listens more
- Asks questions
- Creates trust
- Understands emotions
- Provides solutions
- Guides confidently

If you master sales, you master real estate.

Action Points:

1. **Think Like a Problem-Solver, Not a Seller**
   Focus on understanding needs and offering solutions.
2. **Build Trust Before Pitching Property**
   Connection and comfort come before conversion.
3. **Qualify Every Lead Clearly**
   Ask the right questions to save time and close faster.
4. **Sell Benefits and Emotions, Not Features**
   Connect the property to family security, lifestyle, and future growth.
5. **Use Structured Closing Techniques**
   Guide customers confidently using choice-based and trust-based closes.
6. **Make Site Visits an Experience**
   Plan before, engage during, and follow up immediately after the visit.
7. **Master the Art of Follow-Up**
   Consistent, respectful follow-ups turn interest into bookings.

8

Lead Generation Secrets

*"Lead or Bleed."- **Unknown***

More Leads = More Clients = More Income

Lead generation is the engine of real estate. If leads stop, business stops. If leads double, income doubles. This chapter reveals the most powerful, practical, and proven ways to generate unlimited quality leads in Indian real estate.

7.1 The Truth About Leads

There is no "bad lead". Only "unready lead".

Your job is to connect → nurture → convert.

Every lead is potential money.

7.2 The 4 Types of Real Estate Leads

1. Hot Leads

Ready to buy now (You must close these fast).

2. Warm Leads

Will buy soon (Your follow-up matters).

3. Cold Leads

Interested but not urgent (Nurture them).

4. Referral Leads

Most powerful and easiest to close.
Your growth = Increase hot + warm + referral leads.

7.3 The "10-Source Lead Engine" (IPM System)

Here are the top sources:

1. Instagram Reels

Your strongest weapon. Do 2 reels per day. Topics:

- Property tours
- Price updates
- Investment advice
- Client selfies
- Motivational lines

Reels bring massive inquiries.

2. Facebook Ads

Low cost, high reach. Target:

- Indore
- Dewas
- Ujjain Road
- Super Corridor
- 10–12 km radius around project

Budget: ₹300 to ₹1000/day.

3. Google Ads

People searching "plot in Indore" → instant hot leads.

4. YouTube Videos

Long videos = High trust
High trust = High conversion.

5. WhatsApp Broadcast List

Add 300–500 contacts. Send:

- New project launch
- Offers
- Availability updates

This gives daily 20–30 inquiries.

6. Referral Programs

Give ₹5,000–₹10,000 referral reward. People will start sending leads themselves.

7. Local Events & Seminars

Organize:

- IPM Seminar
- Investment Workshop
- Project Walkthrough Day
- Brokers Meet

Leads come in bulk.

8. Auto-Rickshaw Ads

Low cost, super local reach.

1 auto = 1000+ local eyes daily.

9. Google Business Profile

Optimize with:

- Photos
- Reviews
- Videos
- Offers

This gives organic leads every week.

10. Networking Circles (BNI, Builders, Investors)
Your network multiplies your business 10X.

7.4 The Lead Magnet System (Downloadables)

Create:

- "Indore Property Report"
- "Plot Buying Guide"
- "Investment Tips eBook"
- "Price Trend Analysis"

People give contact numbers to download. You get unlimited leads.

7.5 IPM Formula for Daily Lead Generation

Daily targets:

- 2 reels
- 10 stories
- 1 YouTube short
- 2 broadcast messages
- 20 new contacts
- 1 project update
- 1 testimonial post

Do this → 30–50 leads daily is normal.

7.6 The Power of Follow-Up in Lead Conversion

Lead generation gives you contacts. Follow-up gives you sales. Follow-up timeline:

Day 1 → Call
Day 2 → WhatsApp message
Day 3 → Project brochure

Day 5 → Price update
Day 7 → Site visit invite
Day 10 → Offer
Day 15 → "Last few plots left"
This system converts warm leads into buyers.

7.7 Lead Management System (LMS)

Use tools:
• Excel
• Google Sheets
• CRM apps
• WhatsApp tags
Track:

- New lead
- Interest level
- Site visit done
- Follow-up status
- Closing probability

Organized leads = More bookings.

7.8 Mistakes That Kill Lead Generation

1. Posting irregularly
2. Not using paid ads
3. Low-quality videos
4. No Google reviews
5. Ignoring old leads
6. Not recording site visits

Lead generation is simple...But consistency is rare.

7.9 30-Day Lead Explosion Plan

Week 1 – Social Media Setup

Branding + reels + story posting

Week 2 – Paid Marketing

Facebook + Google ads

Week 3 – Community Building

BNI + seminars + networking

Week 4 – Conversion Week

WhatsApp blasts + urgency offers + last-call follow-ups

This 30-day plan brings 300–800 leads easily.

7.10 Conclusion: Lead Flow = Income Flow

A real estate business grows only when leads flow continuously.

More leads → more site visits

More visits → more bookings

More bookings → more money

Lead generation is not a one-time action. It is a daily discipline. Master this chapter and your pipeline will never drain.

Action Points:

1. **Build daily lead habits** – Post reels, stories, broadcasts, and project updates every single day without breaks.
2. **Use multiple lead sources** – Never depend on one platform; combine social media, ads, referrals, and networking.
3. **Capture and organize every lead** – Track all inquiries in a sheet or CRM with follow-up status.
4. **Follow up with a fixed system** – Call, message, update, and invite consistently until the lead converts.

5. **Focus on consistency, not luck** – Lead flow increases when actions are repeated daily for 30 days straight.

9

Client Trust Psychology

*"Trust is built with consistency." - **Lincoln Chafee***

Real estate selling is not only about showing property. It is about winning the psychology of the buyer. If a buyer trusts you, they will buy even if the plot is 2 km away from their desired location. If they don't trust you, they will reject even the best deal.

8.1 – Why Trust = Transaction

Property is the biggest emotional purchase.

People buy with EMOTION first and JUSTIFICATION later.

• They see future safety

• They imagine their kids and family

• They picture their growth

• They calculate appreciation

Before all of this, they look at you and ask silently:

"Is this person trustworthy?"

8.2 – Foundations of Trust

You build trust through:

1. Clarity – Never hide details.
2. Consistency – Be the same online & offline.

3. Commitment – If you promise, you deliver.
4. Care – Buyers trust those who genuinely care.

8.3 – How to Activate Trust Quickly

Use the 3C Method:

- Connect emotionally
- Comfort the buyer by simplifying the process
- Convince using facts, proof & authority

8.4 – Trust Destroyers

Avoid:

- Overpromising
- Late responses
- Hiding information
- Negative talk about competitors
- Pressure selling

8.5 – Trust Builders

Include:

- Buyer journey videos
- Real client testimonials
- Before–after success examples
- Photos with families on registry day
- Transparent pricing

Remember: Trust takes time to build and seconds to destroy.

Action Points:

1. **Be radically transparent** – Share pricing, documents, timelines, and risks clearly without hiding details.

2. **Respond fast, always** – Quick replies signal reliability and professionalism to buyers.
3. **Show real proof** – Use client testimonials, registry-day photos, and success stories regularly.
4. **Match words with actions** – Deliver exactly what you promise; consistency builds long-term trust.
5. **Sell with care, not pressure** – Guide buyers calmly and confidently, focusing on their family and future.

10

Lead Generation Mastery

*"The money is in the list."- **Russell Brunson***

Without leads, no business survives. With high-quality leads, any business explodes.

9.1 – Organic Lead Sources

- Facebook & Instagram content
- YouTube property reviews
- Google My Business updates
- Local real estate groups
- Community engagement
- Referral network

9.2 – Paid Lead Sources

- Meta ads
- YouTube ads
- Google search ads
- Local newspaper ads
- Radio & outdoor hoardings
- RWA activations

9.3 – The "Lead Magnet" Technique

Offer something valuable free:

- Legal guide
- Discount coupons
- Free site visit
- Market appreciation report

When you give value first... leads start flowing automatically.

9.4 – High-Intent Lead Handling

Once you get a lead:

- Contact within 5 minutes
- Ask relevant questions
- Offer solution-based guidance
- Invite for site visit
- Share proof, photos, videos
- Follow-up until closure

Remember: Follow-up turns "no" into "yes."

Action Points:

1. **Leverage organic sources daily** – Post engaging content on Instagram, Facebook, YouTube, and Google My Business.
2. **Use paid ads strategically** – Run Meta, Google, and YouTube campaigns targeting your hyper-local audience.
3. **Create high-value lead magnets** – Offer guides, site visits, or market reports to attract contacts.
4. **Respond fast to new leads** – Contact within 5 minutes to maximize conversion chances.
5. **Follow-up systematically** – Use calls, WhatsApp, emails, and reminders until the lead is ready to book.

11

Negotiation Power – How to Sell at Your Price

"We're all somebody's prospect; we're all somebody's customer."- ***Chris Murray***

Most agents lose deals because they panic during negotiation.

11.1 – Negotiation Mindset

Always negotiate from a position of confidence, not "desperation."

11.2 – Techniques

- Give value before price
- Offer choices
- Stack benefits
- Show comparisons
- Keep silence after quoting price

11.3 – Walk-Away Power

The strongest negotiation tool: Ability to walk away respectfully. If buyer is serious, they will come back.

Action Points:

1. Prepare Before You Negotiate
2. Lead with Value, Not Price
3. Master the Power of Silence
4. Offer Choices Instead of Ultimatums

12

Mastering Follow-Up

"The answers will be given to those who are bold enough to ask." -
Amit Kalantri

80% sales come from follow-up.

12.1 – Follow-Up Tools

- WhatsApp
- Email
- Calling
- Festive wishes
- Market updates

12.2 – Follow-Up Format

Always:

1. Add value
2. Stay polite
3. Be consistent
4. Never force

Example:

"Sir, I noticed a new appreciation cycle starting on Ujjain Road. Thought this may help in your investment decision."

Soft. Smart. Effective.

Action Points:

1. Accept That Follow-Up Is the Real Sale
2. Build a Multi-Channel Follow-Up System
3. Always Lead with Value
4. Keep the Tone Soft and Respectful
5. Never Force a Decision

13

Building a Real Estate Team – From Solo to Leader

"Coming together is a beginning. Keeping together is progress. Working is success."- ***Henry Ford***

A true entrepreneur grows when he builds a team.

13.1 – Team Structure

- Telecalling
- Closing managers
- Site visit coordinators
- Digital marketing
- CRM team
- Sales executives

13.2 – Training System

Train your team in:

- Projects
- Human psychology
- Negotiation
- Digital tools
- Scripts & pitch

13.3 – Culture of Growth

A team grows when:

• Performance is rewarded
• Mistakes are learned from
• Communication stays open
• Vision stays clear

Action Points:

1. Shift Your Identity from Agent to Leader
2. Build a Clear Team Structure
3. Hire for Attitude, Train for Skill
4. Create a Standard Training Framework
5. Coach Regularly, Not Occasionally

14

Brand Positioning: Becoming No.1 in Your City

*"Your brand is what people say about you when you're not in the room."- **Jeff Bezos***

Your brand is built through:

- Consistency of message
- Client experience
- Digital presence
- Offline visibility
- Project delivery

14.1 – Online Branding

- Daily content
- Testimonials
- Client stories
- Market updates
- Reels + photos

14.2 – Offline Branding

- Hoardings

- Events
- Seminars
- Community activities
- CSR (like Blood Donation, Food Drives)

Action Points:

1. Define One Clear Brand Message
2. Deliver a Remarkable Client Experience
3. Be Visible Every Day, Not Occasionally
4. Create Daily Value-Based Content
5. Use Testimonials as Proof, Not Decoration

15

Technology, Tools & Automation to Grow 10X

*"Set targets 10X bigger than what you believe is possible, and then take 10X the action."- **Grant Cardone***

Use:

- CRM
- Lead tracker
- Bulk WhatsApp tools
- Property videos
- Drone shots
- Google Sheets
- AI for content

If you don't use technology, you will stay behind.

Action Points

1. Adopt a CRM as Your Command Center
2. Automate Lead Management
3. Use Bulk WhatsApp Responsibly

4. Show, Don't Explain, Through Video
5. Centralize Data with Simple Tools

16

Future of Real Estate

*"Ninety percent of all millionaires become so through owning real estate." – **Andrew Carnegie***

The Future of Real Estate:

- Smart townships
- Expressway developments
- High-rise boom
- Investor migration
- NRI interest
- Digital registry
- AI-based valuations

Those who adapt will lead. Those who ignore will disappear.

Action Points:

1. Study Smart Township Models
2. Track Infrastructure-Led Growth Zones
3. Follow Investor Migration Patterns
4. Stay Updated on Digital Registries

5. Educate Clients Continuously
6. Upgrade Skills Every Year

17

Your Personal Growth Journey – The Final Secret

"Unless you try to do something beyond what you have already mastered, you will never grow." -***Ronald Osborn***

Before you grow your business, grow yourself.

Daily Habits

- Read 10 pages
- Learn 30 minutes
- Stay punctual
- Practice discipline
- Review your goals

17.2 – Your Purpose

Real estate is not about selling land.

It is about selling:

- Dreams
- Security
- Future
- Happiness
- Lifestyle

When this becomes your purpose, money follows automatically.

Action Points:

1. Commit to Daily Personal Growth
2. Respect Time and Discipline
3. Review Your Goals Every Day
4. Upgrade Your Mind Before Your Market
5. Define Your Deeper Purpose

18

Conclusion

The Ultimate Growth Formula (IPM Success Code)

This formula can change any real estate career:

Knowledge + Confidence + Consistency + Trust + Team + Technology =Massive, Unstoppable Growth.

You are not just selling property.
You are building cities.
You are shaping families.
You are creating prosperity for generations.
This book is your roadmap...
Your guide...
Your secret weapon.
Now—go and create history.

19

Find Me Here

Instagram Page of Indore Property Management Pvt. Ltd.

Facebook Page of Indore Property Management Pvt. Ltd.

Website of Indore Property Management Pvt. Ltd.

9 789356 198098

Printed at Repro India Ltd.